KU-753-306

Contents

Time to go home

It is Friday and school is over. The children are all looking forward to the weekend. They pack their bags and say goodbye to their friends.

'Before you go,' says Mrs Bennett, their teacher, 'can you remember what I told you about talking to strangers on the way home?' The children all shout together, 'Don't talk to strangers!'

Their teacher laughs. 'Well done!' she says. 'And who is a stranger?' she asks. 'Someone you don't know!' the children shout.
'That's right,' their teacher says. 'Goodbye everyone, and have fun at the weekend.'

SAFETY FIRST

LIBRARY & HERITAGE SERVICE

Online Services
www.kingston.gov.uk

THE ROYAL BOROUGH OF
KINGSTON
UPON THAMES

Renew a book (5 times)
Change of address
Library news and updates
Search the catalogue

Request a book
Email a branch
Get your PIN
Access reference sites

Tolworth Library
37/39 The Broadway
Tolworth
KT6 7DJ
Tel: 020 8547 5006

WITHDRAWN

KT 1044225 1

S   ers

Helena Attlee

Commissioned photography by
Chris Fairclough

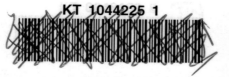

TTS

LONDON • SYDNEY

This edition 2008

Franklin Watts
338 Euston Road, London NW1 3BH

Franklin Watts Australia
Level 17/207 Kent Street, Sydney, NSW 2000

© 2004 Franklin Watts

ISBN: 978 0 7496 7924 8

A CIP catalogue record for this book is available from the British Library

Printed in Malaysia

Planning and production by Discovery Books Limited
Editor: Helena Attlee
Designer: Ian Winton
Consultant: Sergeant Richard Newton, Dorset Police

The author, packager and publisher would like to thank the following people for their
participation in this book: Linda, Jeremy, Stephanie, Edward and William Bloomfield,
and Molly Sharp.

Franklin Watts is a division of Hachette Children's Books, an Hachette Livre UK company.

Mobile phones

Here are Molly and Stephanie. They are both in Mrs Bennett's class at school.

Now that school is over, Stephanie takes out her mobile and turns it on. 'Put your mobile safely away in your bag, Stephanie,' suggests the classroom assistant. 'If you walk around with it in your hand, someone might be tempted to steal it.'

SAFETY FACTS

- Always keep your mobile out of sight, in case someone tries to steal it.
- Try not to use your mobile in the street.

On the way home

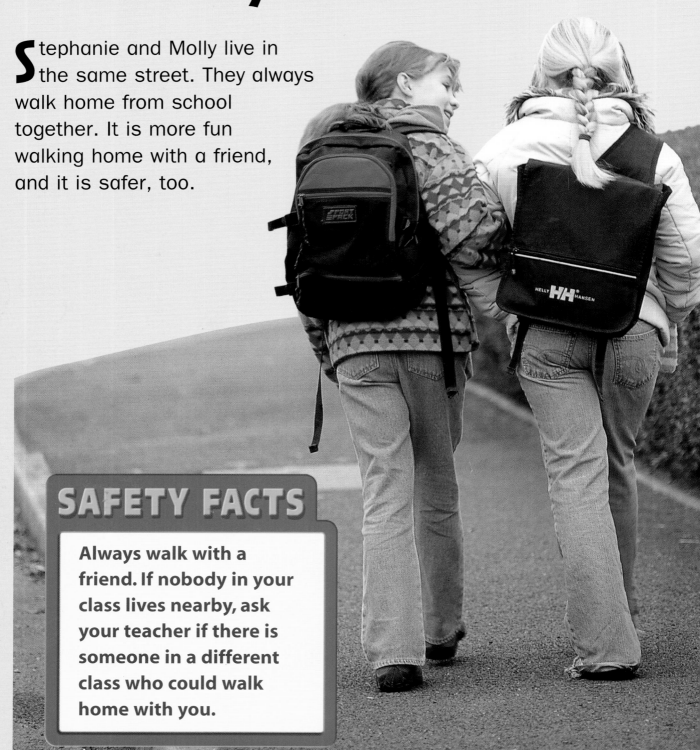

Stephanie and Molly live in the same street. They always walk home from school together. It is more fun walking home with a friend, and it is safer, too.

SAFETY FACTS

Always walk with a friend. If nobody in your class lives nearby, ask your teacher if there is someone in a different class who could walk home with you.

Waiting for Mum

As the girls walk out of the school gates they see their friend William waiting for his Mum to collect him in the car.

'You can walk home with us if you like, William,' suggests Molly. 'Thanks Molly,' says William, 'but I'd better not. My Mum is coming to collect me, and she would be worried if I wasn't here.'

SAFETY FACTS

- Always have a plan, and let the grown-up who looks after you know what it is.
- Never change your plan at the last minute.
- If something unexpected happens and you have to change your plan, ring home to tell your parents what you are doing.

Sticking together

On the way home, Molly and Stephanie walk past the park. They see their friend Edward playing on the climbing frame. 'Come and join me,' he shouts.

'Why don't we stop and play for a bit?' asks Molly. 'We'll see my Mum if she comes, so she won't worry about us.'
'Sorry, Molly,' says Stephanie. 'I need to get home, and I can't go without you because we aren't allowed to split up.'

SAFETY FACTS

- Never split up when you are supposed to be walking home together.
- Do not stop to play on your way home.

Making plans

Molly and Stephanie wave to Edward. They decide to come back to the park tomorrow.

'Let's ask Edward to come too,' suggests Stephanie. 'I'll ask my Dad to ring up tonight and arrange it.'

'Tell him to bring his football!' Molly says, happily.

SAFETY FACTS

Make sure that your parents or carers know about the arrangements you have made with your friends.

A stranger in a car

Molly and Stephanie have to walk up a steep hill on their way home.
'Phew!' puffs Stephanie. 'I'm tired.'
Just then, a car pulls up beside them. 'Hello you two,' says the lady driver. 'Would you like a lift home?'
'No thanks!' Stephanie and Molly answer together.
The lady smiles, and then she waves to them as she drives off.

'Who was that?' asks Molly.
'I think she has just moved into our street,' Stephanie replies, 'but I don't know her name.'

SAFETY FACTS

- **Never go anywhere with a stranger.**
- **Never accept a lift in a car from a stranger.**

The right thing to do

Stephanie is worried. 'I hope she won't think we are rude,' she says to Molly.

'Nice grown-ups never mind when you say "no",' Molly tells her. 'That's what Mrs Bennett said at school today.'

As the girls reach the top of the hill, they see Molly's Mum walking towards them. They tell her about the lady offering them a lift.

'Well done, girls,' Mum says. 'That was the right thing to do.'

Strangers on the internet

When Stephanie gets home she has tea with her Dad. After tea, Stephanie asks if she can go on the computer. 'Of course,' says Dad, 'but what do you want to do on it?'

Stephanie explains that she wants to go to an online chat room. She made a friend there last week, and she had great fun chatting to her. She wants to chat to her again, today.

'That's fine, Stephanie,' says Dad, 'but remember, she's not a real friend because you haven't really met her.'

Pretending to be someone else

'But I know all about her!' cries Stephanie. 'She's called Jess, she's my age, and she likes riding and football, just like me. She has even sent me a picture of herself on her pony!'

'That's lovely, Stephanie,' Dad says. 'But remember, on the internet people can pretend to be someone else.'

SAFETY FACTS

- Do not think of the people you chat with online as people you really know. They are still strangers.
- Tell the adult looking after you all about the people you meet on the internet, and let them read their messages.

Staying safe on the internet

When Stephanie has been on the internet for a few minutes, Dad comes in to see how she is getting on.

'Dad,' says Stephanie, 'I've been chatting to Jess and she says that she would like to meet me. She only lives on the other side of town. Could we meet up at the weekend?'

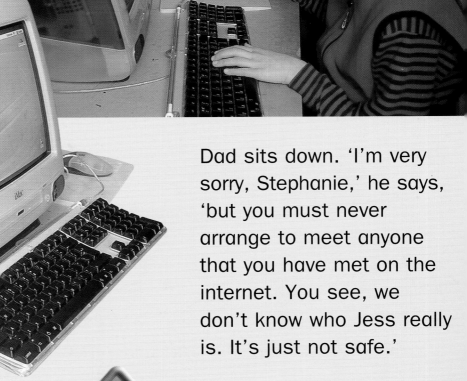

Dad sits down. 'I'm very sorry, Stephanie,' he says, 'but you must never arrange to meet anyone that you have met on the internet. You see, we don't know who Jess really is. It's just not safe.'

Stephanie chats to Jess for a bit longer. Then she turns off the computer and goes downstairs. She asks her Dad to ring up Edward's Mum, and arrange for them to meet in the park tomorrow.

'All right,' says Dad. 'We certainly know that Edward really is who he says he is! I'll ring his Mum straight away.'

'Tell him to bring his football!' laughs Stephanie.

SAFETY FACTS

- Never arrange to see anyone you have met online. IT IS NOT SAFE!

Not their business

It is Saturday morning, and Stephanie has just finished breakfast. She is thinking about Jess, the girl she met on the internet. She still doesn't understand why her Dad won't allow them to meet.

'I know, Dad,' she suggests, 'why don't I arrange to meet Jess here, and then you could see her, too? I've told her all about our cat, and she wants to see him.'

'I'm sorry, Stephanie,' Dad says again. 'I know it is a shame, but you really do have to be careful about the internet.'

Sometimes nasty grown-ups use the internet as a way of getting to know children. You can never tell who you are really chatting to on the internet. That is why you must never give out your address. It is not their business!

SAFETY FACTS

Never tell someone you have met on the internet:
• Your address.
• Your telephone number.
• The name of your school.
IT IS NOT SAFE!

Going shopping

After breakfast, Molly and Stephanie go to the shops at the end of their road. Molly wants to buy a get-well card for her Granny.
'Don't talk to anyone that you don't know, and come straight home,' says Stephanie's Dad.
'Stay together all the time,' says Molly's Mum.

Disaster!

Molly finds a lovely card. She is about to pay for it, but when she puts her hand in her pocket, her purse is not there!
'Oh no!' says Molly.
'I must have dropped my purse.' She starts to cry.

A man sees Molly crying. He comes over to her and says kindly, 'Shall I lend you some money? I work with your Dad, and he could pay me back on Monday.'

Molly and Stephanie look at each other. They do not know the man, and they do know that they must not take anything from a stranger. 'No thanks!' they say.

SAFETY FACTS

Never accept money, sweets or anything else from a stranger.

Strangers you can trust

Molly and Stephanie are not sure what to do. They are in trouble. They do not know anybody in the shop, but they need help. Sometimes you have to talk to strangers, and then you should look around for someone you can trust. Perhaps there is a shop nearby, where your parents know the shopkeeper.

If you have to ask a stranger for help, don't hold hands with them, or go anywhere with them.

SAFETY FACTS

Grown-ups you can trust:

- A police officer.
- A school crossing patrol.
- A shopkeeper that your parents know.
- A teacher.
- A doctor.
- A grandparent or other relative.

Getting help

'I know,' says Stephanie, 'let's tell the lady at the till what has happened.'
When they tell the lady at the till about Molly's purse, she starts to smile.

'That's lucky,' she says. 'Someone found the purse on the floor and handed it in just now.'
Molly and Stephanie start to smile, too. Molly pays for the card, and then the girls go straight home.

Telling Mum

When Molly gets home she tells Mum what happened. Mum gives her a drink and a biscuit, and then sits down at the table with her.

'Well done, Molly,' she says. 'You and Stephanie did exactly the right thing.'

'He did look like a very kind man,' explains Molly, 'and he said that he works with Dad.'

'I expect he was kind,' replies Mum, 'but you didn't know him.'

'No, I didn't,' agrees Molly, 'and you've told me never to accept anything from a stranger.'

'Well done!' says Mum. 'I'm glad you told me what happened.'

Molly finishes her juice. Then she goes upstairs to her room to write in the card she has bought for her Granny.

SAFETY FACTS

- Although most grown-ups are kind, some may be nasty and they could hurt you.
- If a grown-up ever says or does anything that makes you feel unsafe, always tell your parents or another grown-up you can trust, like your teacher, as soon as you can.

Going to the park

In the afternoon, Molly and Stephanie go to the park to meet Edward. First they go on the swings, and then they play with Edward's football.

While they are playing, Stephanie notices their friend William. He is playing all by himself on the other side of the park. 'William!' they shout, but William does not hear them.

'Come on!' Stephanie says. 'Let's go and go and get him. My Dad says it's not safe to play on your own in the park.'

Before they reach William, a man walks over and starts to play football with him. He kicks the ball to William, and William looks pleased to have someone to play with.
'I'm Tim,' says the man. 'What's your name?'
William never has a chance to reply because suddenly his friends arrive.

SAFETY FACTS

Always go to the park with some friends. Don't play alone.

'Come on,' yells Edward, 'I need you on my team!'
The man goes away without saying goodbye.
'Oh dear,' says William.
'Never mind,' Stephanie tells him. 'If he's a nice man, he will understand – it's always more fun to play with your real friends.'

Runaway dog

The children walk back to the middle of the park and start to play football. Suddenly, a dog runs up and starts to play, too.

'Isn't he sweet!' says Stephanie. The dog's owner watches them playing together. 'Don't let him spoil your football,' she smiles.

The runaway dog

Suddenly the dog runs off into the field next to the park.
'Oh no,' his owner cries. 'Now he will get lost! Can you
come and help me get him back?'
The children look at each other. The woman is
a stranger, and they know that they must never
go anywhere with strangers.
'We're really sorry,' says Edward,
'but we have to go home now
because it will be dark soon.'

SAFETY FACTS

Don't go anywhere
with a stranger.

Getting home

Edward's house is next to the park. Stephanie and Molly walk with him to his front door.

'Goodbye, Edward,' say the girls. 'See you at school on Monday.'

It is beginning to get dark now. William, Stephanie and Molly hurry along the road towards home. They know that they must get there before nightfall. Their parents will start to worry about them soon.

They have been told that it is dangerous to stay out after dark.

A short cut

When Stephanie walks along this road with her Dad, they sometimes take a short cut along an alley. When they reach the entrance to the alley, Stephanie suggests, 'Let's take the short cut.'

Molly is not sure this is a good idea.
'Better not,' she says. 'Mum told me that I should always stay on the main roads.'
'All right,' agrees Stephanie, 'but we'll have to run if we want to get home before dark.'

William, Stephanie and Molly reach home safely, just before it gets dark.

SAFETY FACTS

Don't take short cuts. Stay on well-lit streets where there are plenty of people.

Glossary

Alley Narrow path or passage.

Arrangements Plans, usually made with other people.

Carer Someone who looks after you.

Chat room Internet site where you can 'chat' with other people by sending written messages.

Classroom assistant Person who helps the teacher in the classroom.

Internet The worldwide network of millions of connected computers.

Online On the internet.

School crossing patrol Person who helps schoolchildren to cross the road safely.

Shopkeeper Someone who works in a shop.

Short cut Route that gets you to your destination more quickly than the usual one.

Stranger Someone you don't know, although not all nasty adults are strangers.

Useful addresses and websites

BBC
www.bbc.co.uk/chatguide
A site designed for use by children, adolescents and parents. It is full of information and advice about safety while chatting online.

Child Alert
www.childalert.co.uk
Information on keeping children safe and well. Publishes the Be Safe guides about internet and mobile phone safety.

ChildLine
www.childline.org.uk
ChildLine is the free 24-hour helpline for children and young people in the UK. Children and young people can call the helpline on 0800 1111 about any problem, at any time - day or night.

Kidsmart
www.kidsmart.org.uk
A practical internet safety advice website for pupils, parents and teachers and schools, focusing on the internet and mobile phones - whether used at school or in the home.

NCH
www.nch.org.uk/information/index.php?i=209
Guides and other resources for how to use the internet safely.

NSPCC
www.nspcc.org.uk
The website includes valuable information on ensuring that your child uses the internet safely.

Parent Centre
www.parentcentre.gov.uk
The latest information and advice for parents and carers on internet safety for children.

Parents Online
www.parents.org.uk
Information on internet safety, learning sites, competitions and events.

Safekids
www.safekids.co.uk
Provides tips and advice on staying safe in many different situations.

Think You Know – chat room safety
www.thinkuknow.co.uk
Site designed for use by children, outlining the dangers of giving out personal information in chat rooms, with easy to follow guidelines.

The Child Accident Prevention Foundation
www.kidsafe.com.au
A nationwide Australian charity providing advice on the prevention of accidents in the home.

Child and Youth Health,
www.cyh.com
295 South Terrace, Adelaide, SA 5000, Australia
Tel +618 8303 1500. Fax +618 8303 1656.
Online resources and links for the latest news and advice about parenting and child safety issues.

Child Safety Foundation
www.childsafety.co.nz
A New Zealand website designed mainly for use by parents, which promotes all aspects of pre-school and early primary school safety.

Note to parents and teachers
Every effort has been made by the Publishers to ensure that these websites are suitable for children, that they are of the highest educational value, and that they contain no inappropriate or offensive material. However, because of the nature of the internet, it is impossible to guarantee that the content of these sites will not be altered. We strongly advise that internet access is supervised by a responsible adult.

Index